AF598972

American Sign Language

Family and Friends

by E. Russell Primm III • illustrated by Kathleen Petelinsek

childsworld.com

Published by The Child's World®
800-599-READ • childsworld.com

Photography Credits
Ground Picture/Shutterstock.com, cover, 17; santypan/Shutterstock.com, 1, 15; pixelheadphoto digitalskillet/Shutterstock.com, 3; Glaze Image/Shutterstock.com, 4; Mladen Zivkovic/Shutterstock.com, 5; Brian Scott Smith/Shutterstock.com, 6; lunamarina/Shutterstock.com, 7; Geoffrey Clowes/Shutterstock.com, 8; Leonard Zhukovsky/Shutterstock.com, 9; Monkey Business Images/Shutterstock.com, 10, 21; George Rudy/Shutterstock.com, 11; Amalia Zilio/Shutterstock.com, 12; Sergey Novikov/Shutterstock.com, 13; Mila Supinskaya Glashchenko/Shutterstock.com, 14; Asia Images Group/Shutterstock.com, 16; Clovera/Shutterstock.com, 18; paulaphoto/Shutterstock.com, 19; fizkes/Shutterstock.com, 20

ISBN Information
9781503889002 (Reinforced Library Binding)
9781503890084 (Portable Document Format)
9781503891326 (Online Multi-user eBook)
9781503892569 (Electronic Publication)

LCCN 2023950261

Printed in the United States of America

Note to Parents, Caregivers, and Educators: The understanding of any language begins with the acquisition of vocabulary, whether the language is spoken or manual. The books in this series provide readers, both young and old, with basic American Sign Language signs. Combining close photo cues and simple, but detailed, line illustrations, children and adults alike can begin the process of learning American Sign Language.

Let these books be an introduction to the world of American Sign Language. Most languages have regional dialects and multiple ways of expressing the same thought. This is also true for sign language. We have attempted to use the most common version of the signs for the words in this series. As with any language, the best way to learn is to be taught in person by a frequent user. It is our hope that this series will pique your interest in sign language.

A special thanks to our advisers: As a member of a deaf family that spans four generations, **Kim Bianco Majeri** lives, works, and plays among the Deaf community. **Carmine L. Vozzolo** is an educator of children who are deaf and hard of hearing, as well as their families.

E. Russell Primm III was a well-known figure in the publishing industry who produced thousands of acclaimed books for children. He was affiliated with organizations such as the American Library Association, the Chicago Book Clinic, and the University of Chicago Publishing Program Advisory Board.

Kathleen Petelinsek has loved books since she was a child. Through the years, she has written, designed, and illustrated many books for children. She lives in Wisconsin, near her granddaughter who also shares her love for books.

A family can have lots of different members.

Family

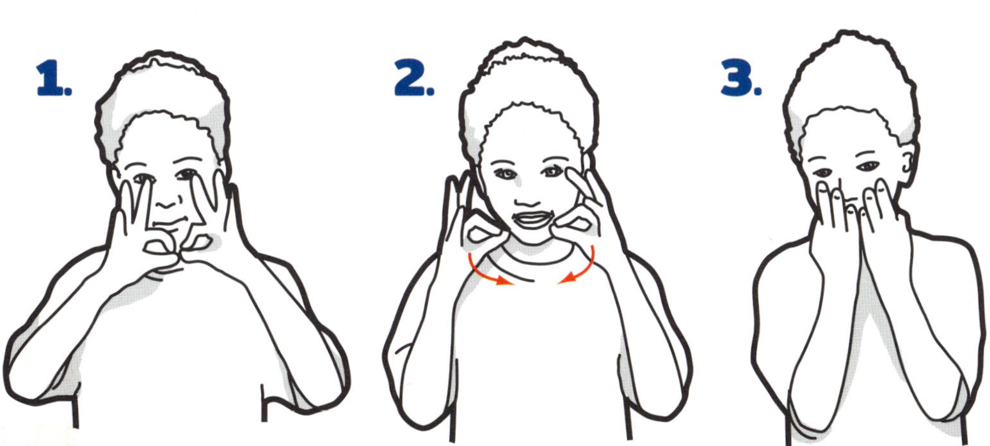

Make the "F" sign with both hands facing each other. Then roll your wrists so that your pinkies touch.

Some people call their mothers "Mom," "Mommy," or "Mama."

Mother

Tap your chin twice with your thumb.

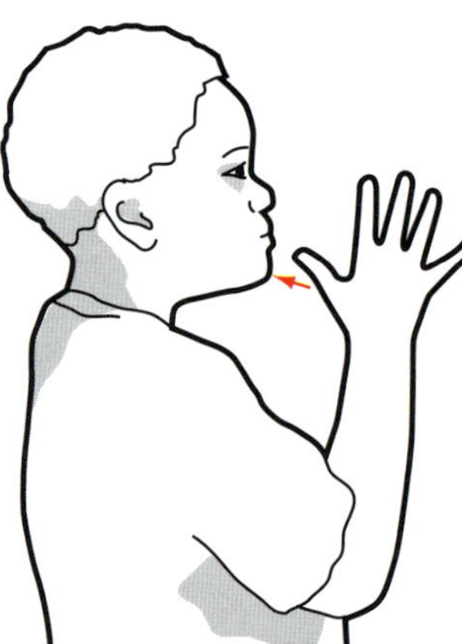

Some people call their fathers "Dad," "Daddy," or "Papa."

Father

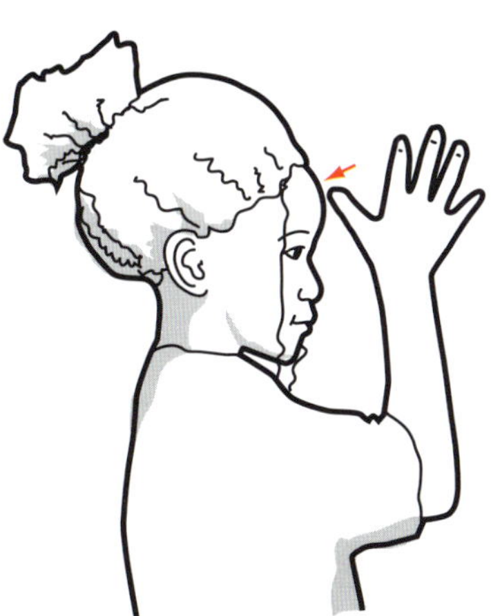

Tap your forehead twice with your thumb.

In Spanish, the word son is *hijo* (EE-ho).

Son

Start with your right hand in a salute. Move your hand down to end as if you are holding a baby.

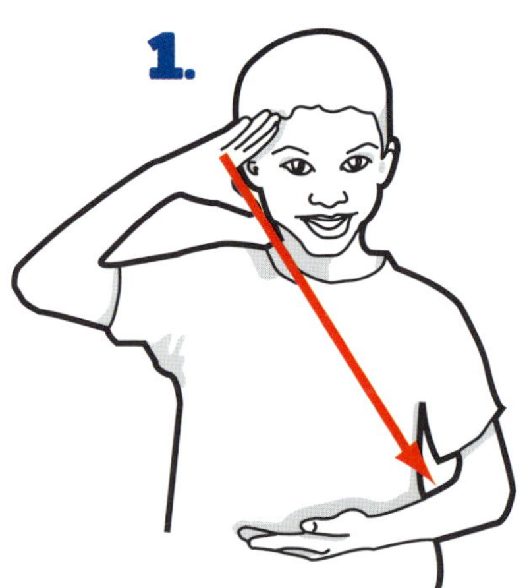

In Spanish, the word daughter is *hija* (EE-ha).

Daughter

1.

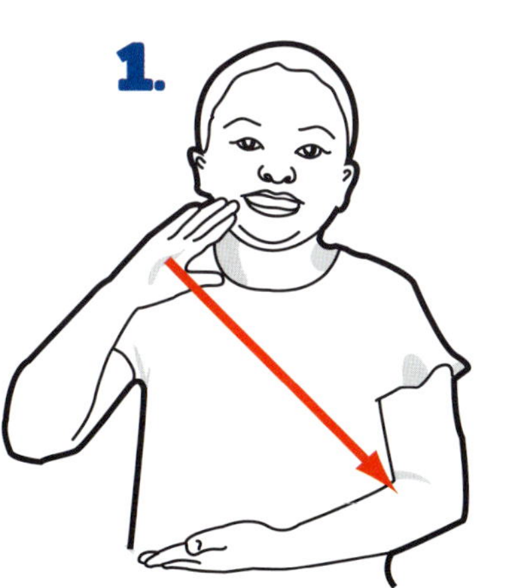

2.

Start with your right hand touching your chin. Move your hand down to end as if you are holding a baby.

Nick, Joe, and Kevin Jonas are famous brothers. Their band, Jonas Brothers, is very popular.

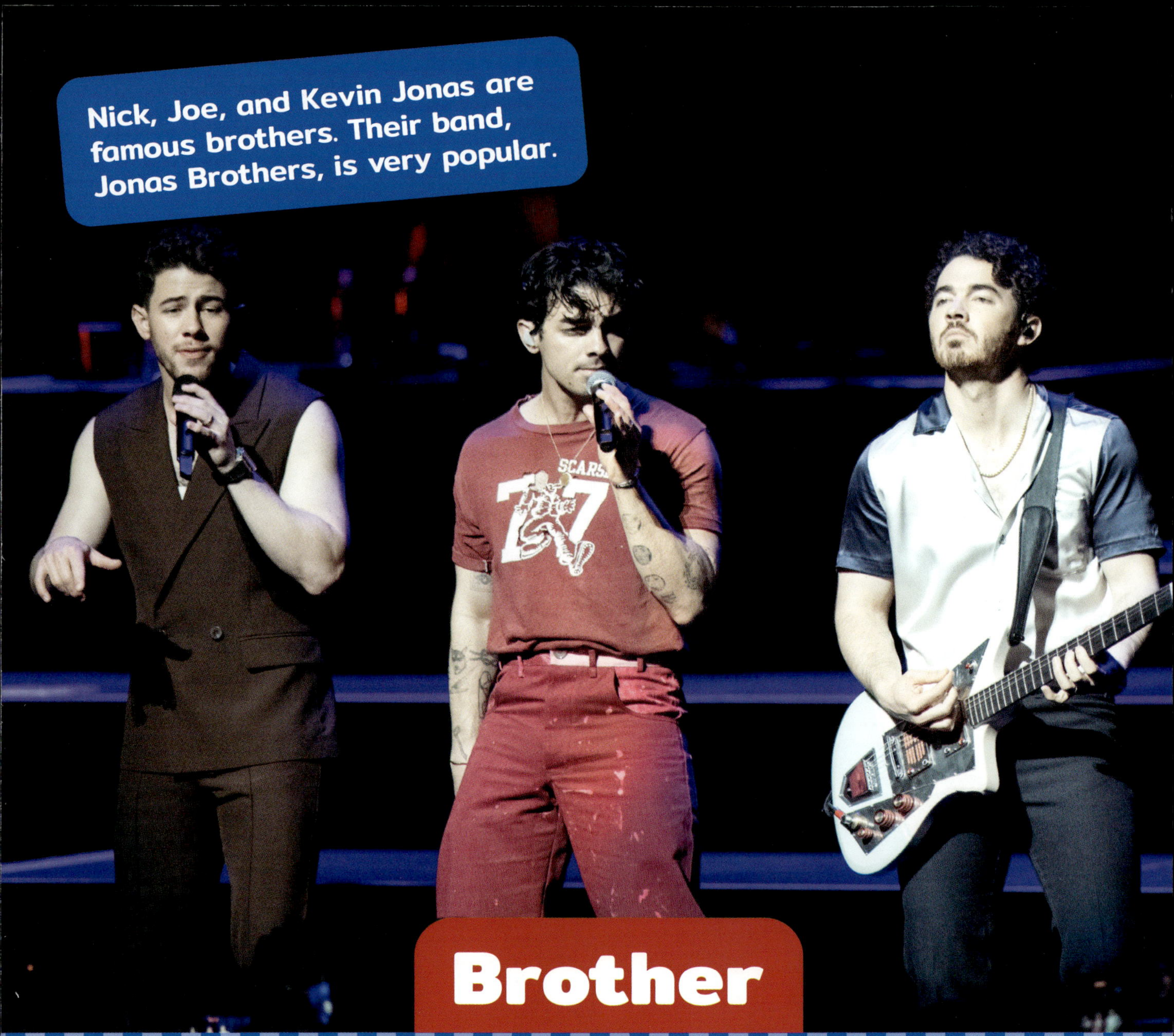

Brother

Both hands make the "L" sign. Touch your right hand to your forehead, then move down until your right wrist rests on your left.

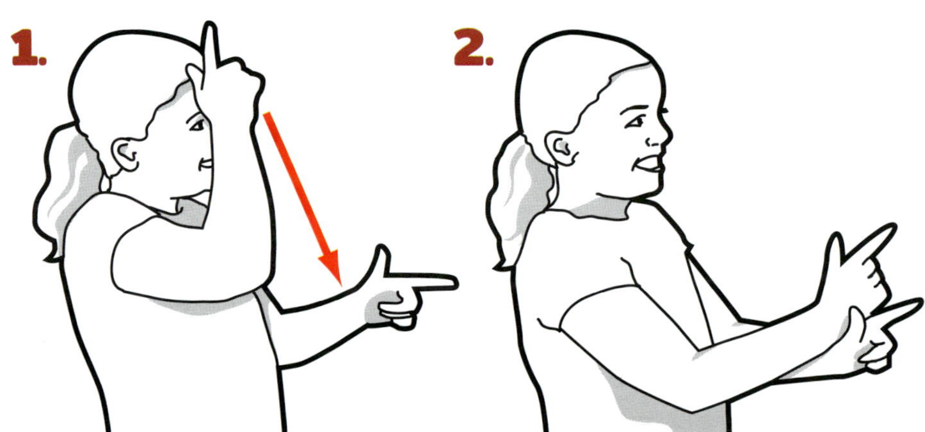

Two famous sisters are Serena and Venus Williams. They are tennis champions.

Sister

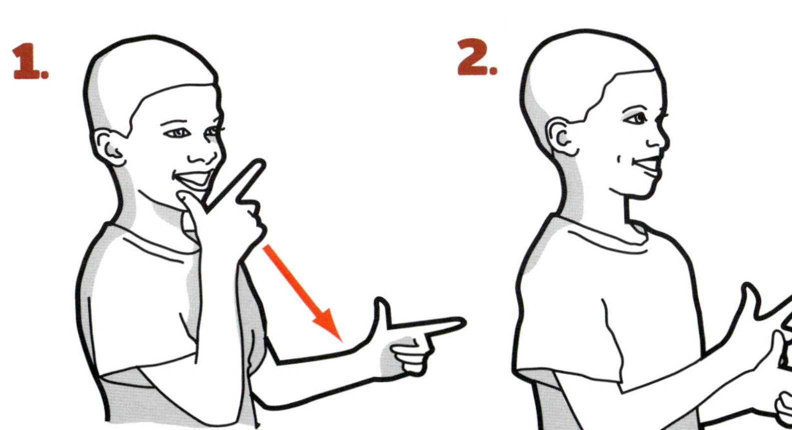

Both hands make the "L" sign. Touch your right hand to your chin, then move down until your right wrist rests on your left.

Most babies start to crawl between seven and twelve months old.

Baby

Swing your arms back and forth as if you were rocking a baby.

Many people look like their parents.

Parent

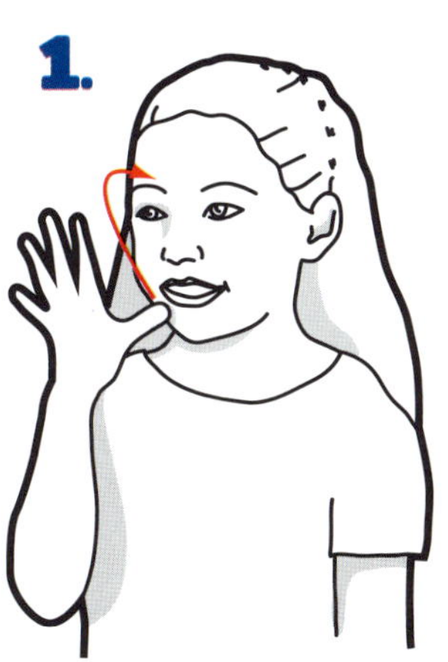

Touch your thumb to your chin. Then quickly touch your thumb to your forehead.

In French, the word child is *enfant* (AHN-fahn).

Child

Motion your hand downward twice. Pretend as if you are patting a child on the head.

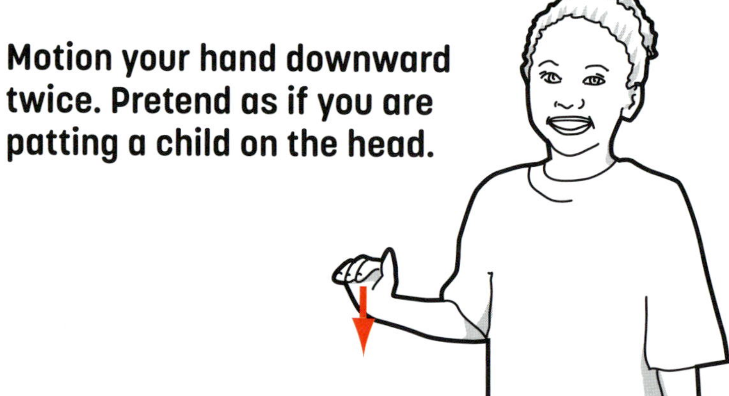

Many children love going to a playground.

Children

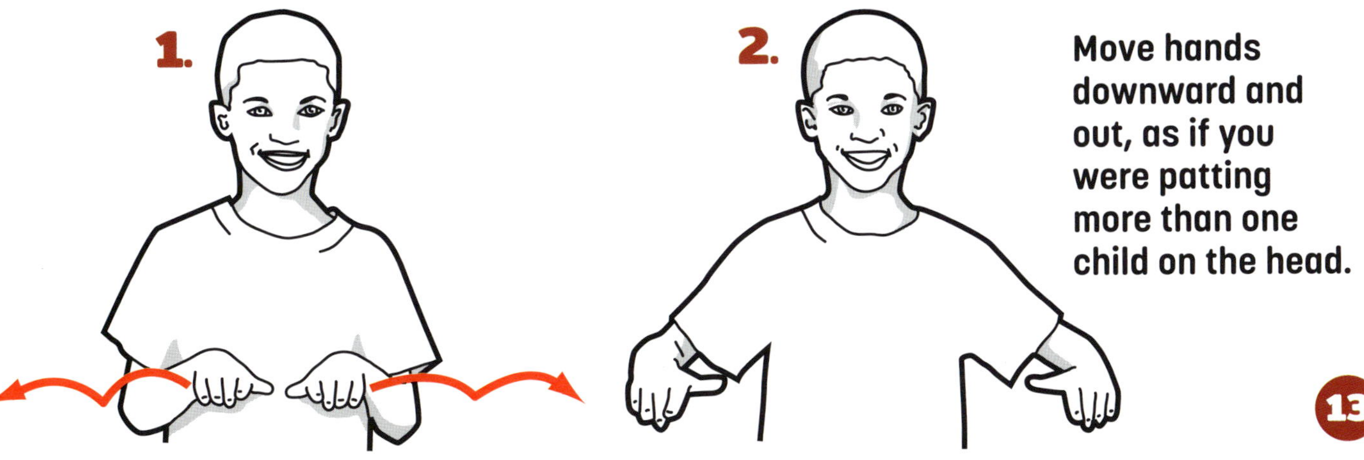

Move hands downward and out, as if you were patting more than one child on the head.

Your aunt is the sister of either your mom or dad.

Aunt

Make the "A" sign with your right hand. Twist your wrist a few times near your cheek.

Your uncle is the brother of either your mom or dad.

Uncle

Make the "U" sign with your right hand. Hold your hand close to your right temple and twist your wrist a few times.

Some people call their grandmothers "Grandma," "Nana," or "Abuela."

Grandmother

Touch your thumb to your chin. Bounce your hand outward twice.

Some people call their grandfathers "Grandpa," "Papa," or "Abuelo."

Grandfather

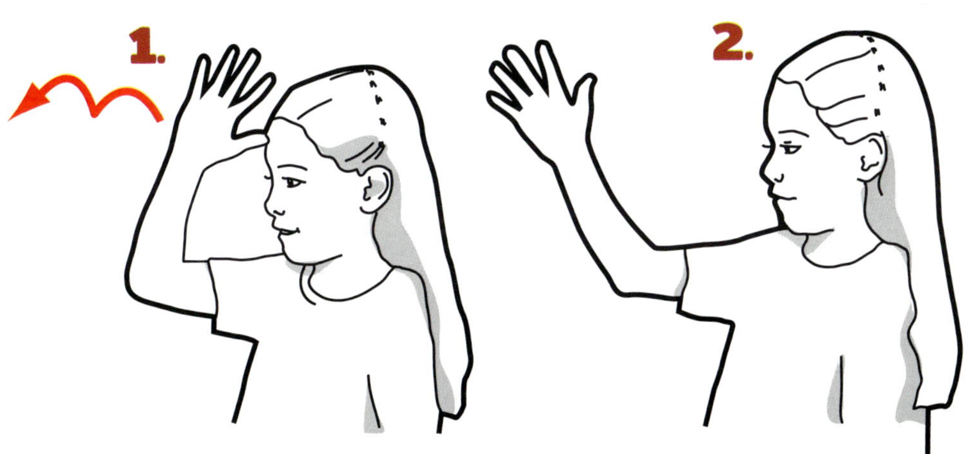

Touch your thumb to your forehead. Bounce your hand outward twice.

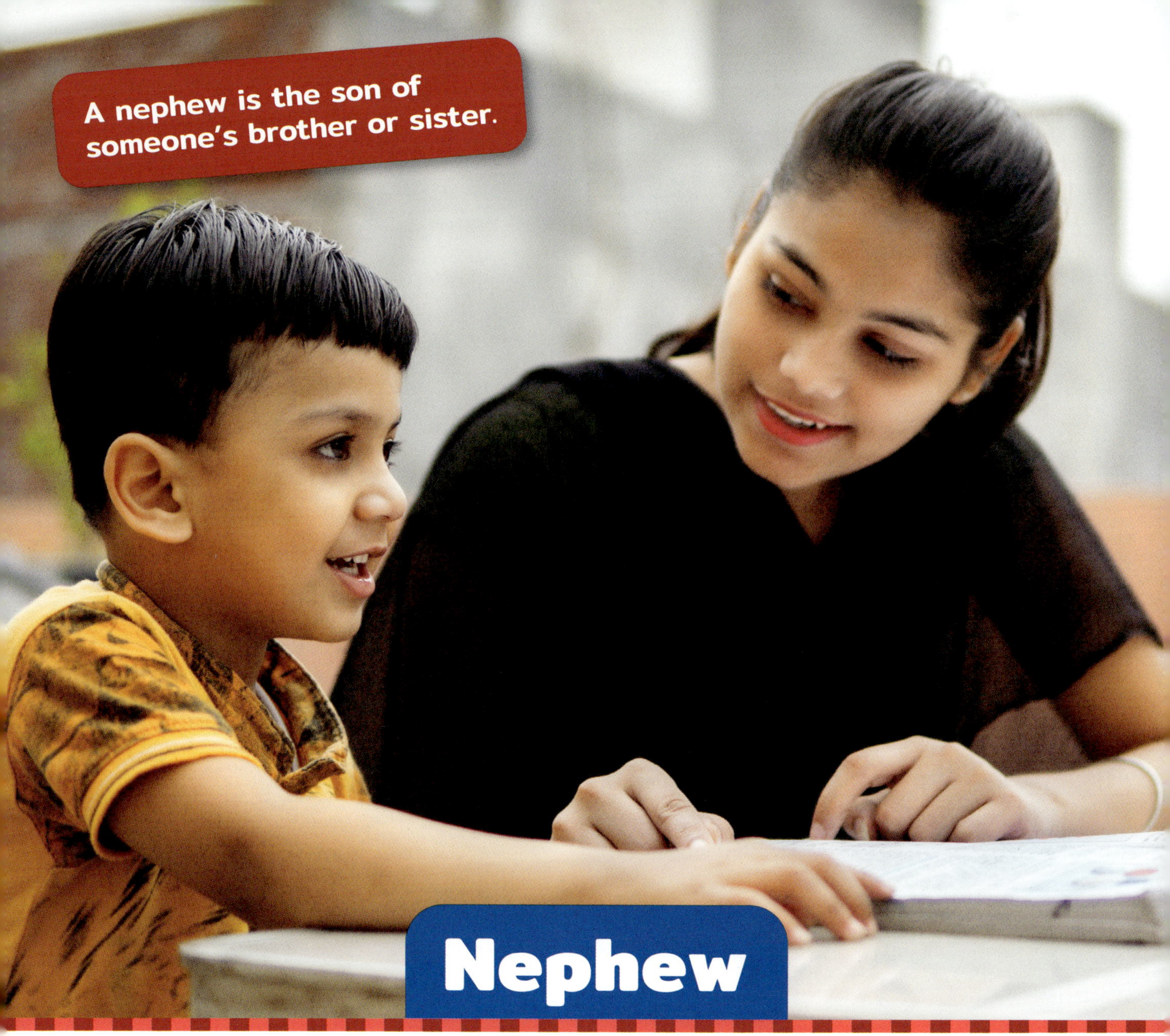

A nephew is the son of someone's brother or sister.

Nephew

Make the "N" sign with your right hand. Twist your wrist near your right eye.

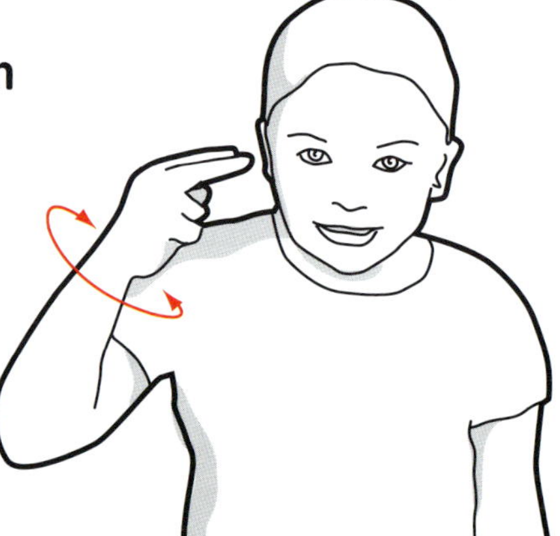

A niece is the daughter of someone's brother or sister.

Niece

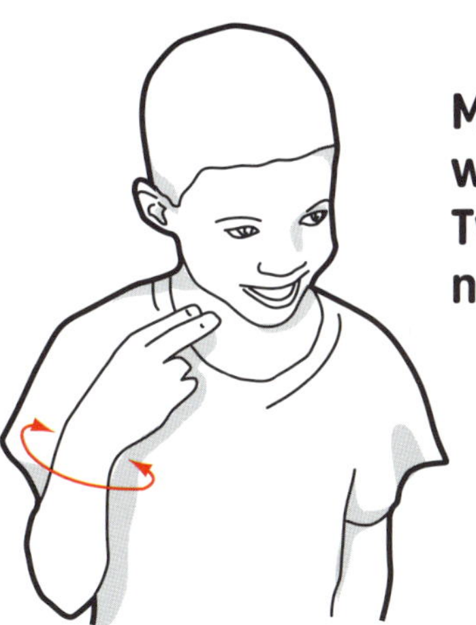

Make the "N" sign with your right hand. Twist your wrist near your right jaw.

Your cousin is the child of your uncle or aunt.

Cousin

Make the "C" sign with your right hand. Shake or twist your wrist near your cheek.

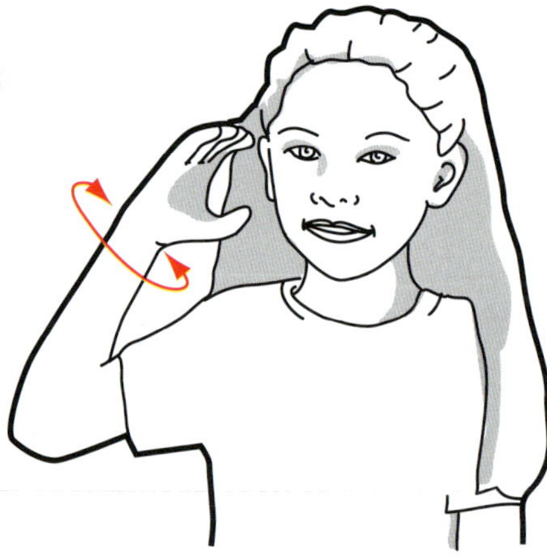

Having a friend can make you feel happy.

Friend

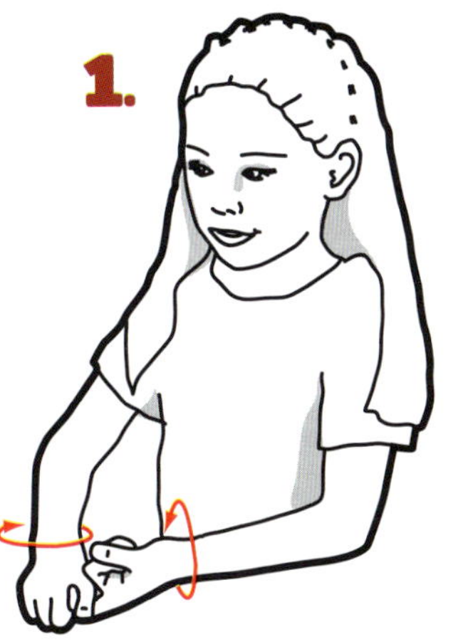

Twist your index fingers together with your right finger on top. Take them apart and put them back together—this time with the left finger on top.

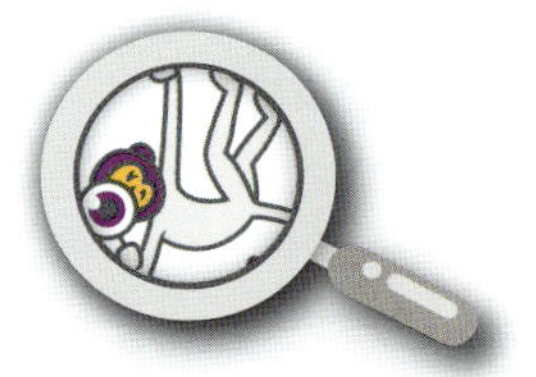

Wonder More

- How much did you know about American Sign Language (ASL) before reading this book? Do you already know some ASL signs? What new signs did you learn?
- Some words or specific names don't have signs. In these cases, you can spell the individual letters of the word, which is called fingerspelling. Look at the alphabet chart on page 23. Can you sign the letters in your name?
- With a partner, pick three signs from this book and practice them together. Are you able to understand each other? Is ASL easier or harder than you thought it would be?
- Think of a word related to family or friends that isn't included in this book. Try signing the word with fingerspelling. Then look up the ASL sign for the word. Where can you find more ASL signs?

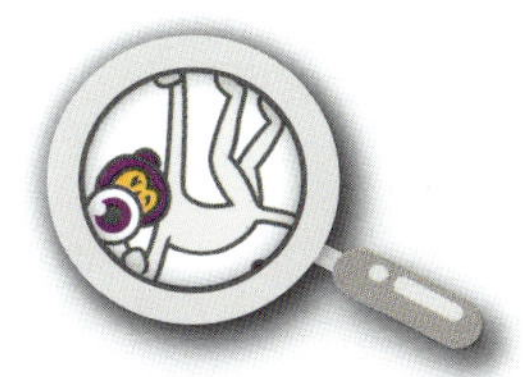

Sign Language Alphabet

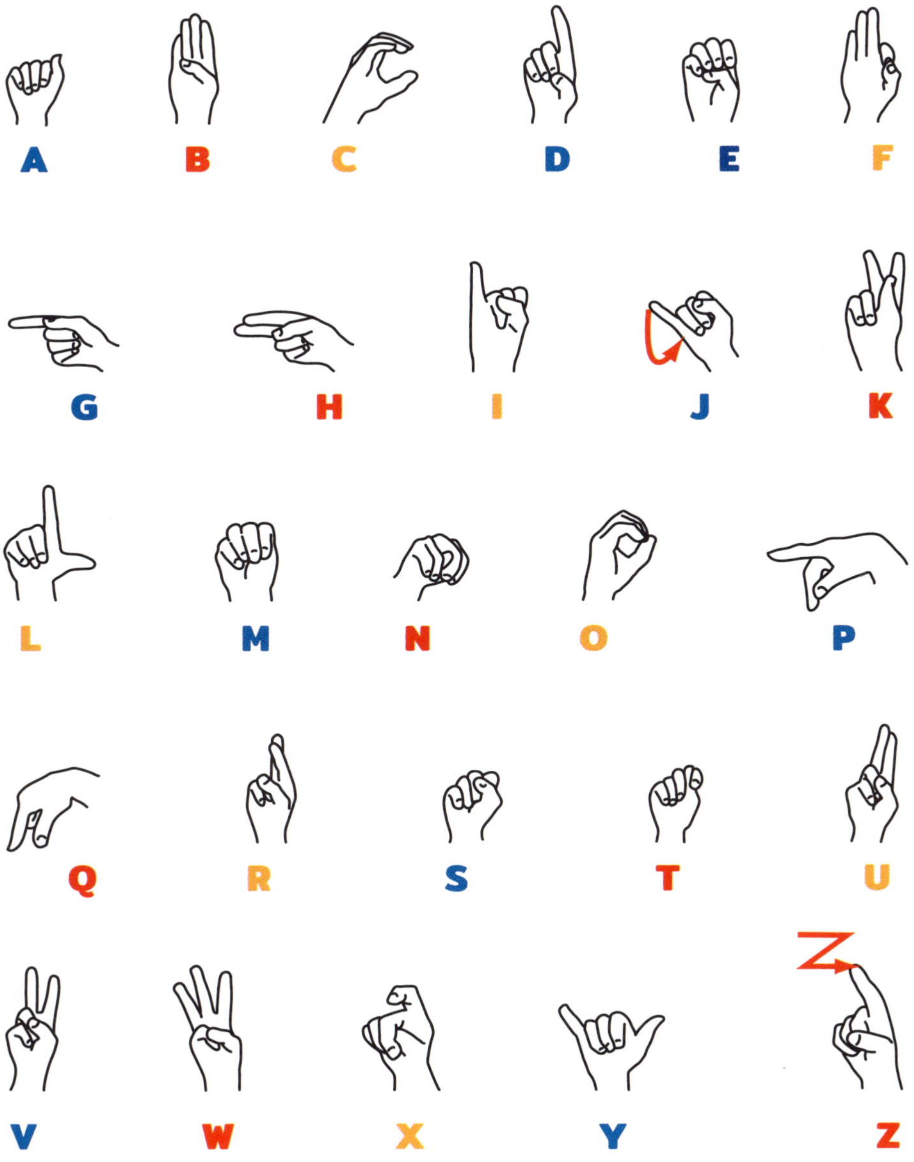

A B C D E F

G H I J K

L M N O P

Q R S T U

V W X Y Z

Find Out More

In the Library

Brakenhoff, Kelly, and Caterina Baldi (illustrator). *Sometimes I Like the Quiet (Duke the Deaf Dog ASL Series)*. Lincoln, NE: Emerald Prairie Press, 2022.

Gallaudet University Press (editor). *The Gallaudet Children's Dictionary of American Sign Language*. Washington, DC: Gallaudet University Press, 2014.

On the Web

Visit our website for links about American Sign Language:
childsworld.com/links

Note to Parents, Caregivers, Teachers, and Librarians: We routinely verify our web links to make sure they are safe and active sites. So encourage your readers to check them out!

A Special Thank-You!

Thank you to our models from the Program for Children Who are Deaf and Hard of Hearing at the Alexander Graham Bell School in Chicago, Illinois.

Alina's favorite things to do are art, soccer, and swimming. DJ is her brother!

Dareous likes football. His favorite team is the Detroit Lions. He also likes to play video games.

Darionna likes the swings and merry-go-round on the playground. She also loves art.

DJ loves playing the harmonica and video games. Alina is his sister!

Jasmine likes writing and math in school. She also loves to swim.